Castle
The Siege Chronicles

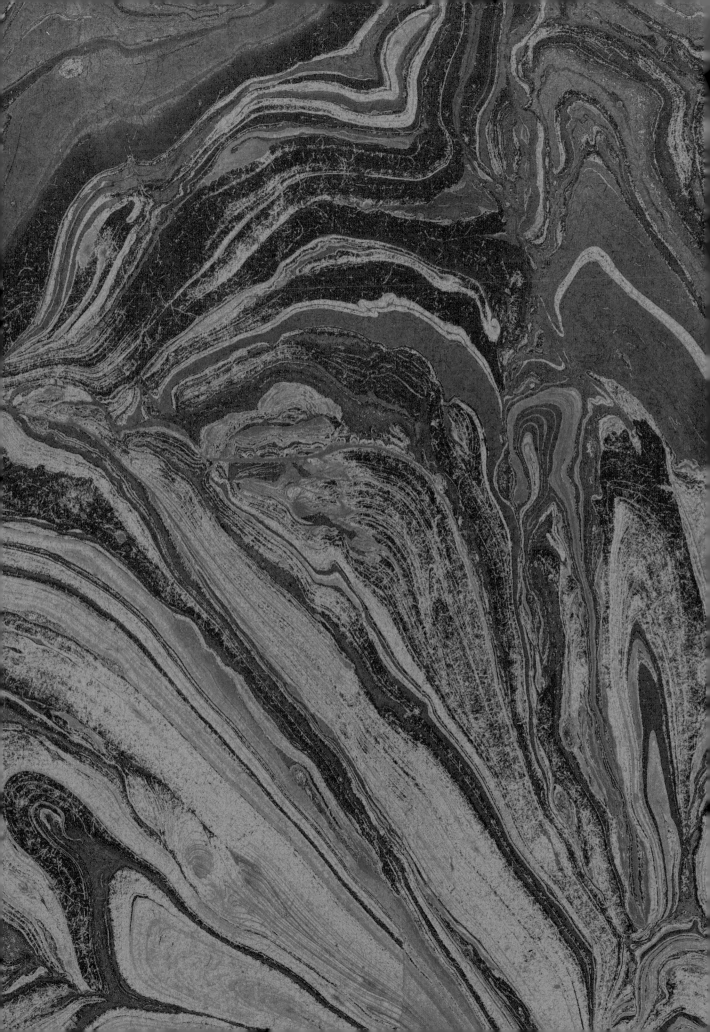

Published by **S**SCRIBO
25 Marlborough Place, Brighton BN1 1UB
A division of Book House, an imprint of
The Salariya Book Company Ltd
www.salariya.com
www.book-house.co.uk

SALARIYA

1 3 5 7 9 8 6 4 2

A CIP catalogue record for this book is available
from the British Library.

Printed and bound in China.
Printed on paper from sustainable sources.This book is sold
subject to the conditions that it shall not, by way of trade or
otherwise, be lent, resold, hired out, or otherwise circulated
without the publisher's prior consent in any form or binding or
cover other than that in which it is published and without
similar condition being imposed
on the subsequent purchaser.

PB ISBN-13: 978-1-910706-00-8

Created and designed by: David Salariya
Editor: Stephen Haynes
Editorial Assistants: Rob Walker, Mark Williams

PAPER FROM
SUSTAINABLE
FORESTS

Visit our web site at **www.book-house.co.uk**
for **free** electronic versions of:
You Wouldn't Want to be an Egyptian Mummy!
You Wouldn't Want to be a Roman Gladiator!
Avoid Joining Shackleton's Polar Expedition!
Avoid Sailing on a 19th-Century Whaling Ship!

Castle
The Siege Chronicles

Derek Farmer

Illustrated by Mark Bergin

Contents

London

ENGLAND

NORMANDY

Rouen

Château-Gaillard   Paris

FRANCE

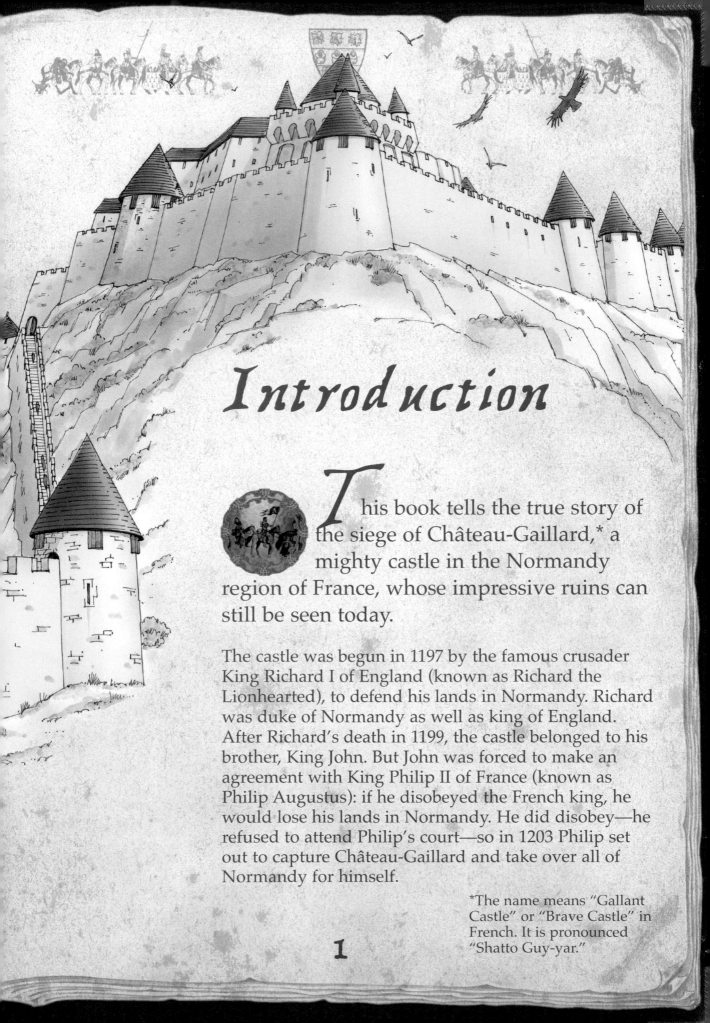

Introduction

*T*his book tells the true story of the siege of Château-Gaillard,* a mighty castle in the Normandy region of France, whose impressive ruins can still be seen today.

The castle was begun in 1197 by the famous crusader King Richard I of England (known as Richard the Lionhearted), to defend his lands in Normandy. Richard was duke of Normandy as well as king of England. After Richard's death in 1199, the castle belonged to his brother, King John. But John was forced to make an agreement with King Philip II of France (known as Philip Augustus): if he disobeyed the French king, he would lose his lands in Normandy. He did disobey—he refused to attend Philip's court—so in 1203 Philip set out to capture Château-Gaillard and take over all of Normandy for himself.

*The name means "Gallant Castle" or "Brave Castle" in French. It is pronounced "Shatto Guy-yar."

1

The Castle

Most castles in the Middle Ages were built by kings or by the rich lords who backed them.

War and peace

In peacetime, the castle's towers and walls were a sign of the owner's power. The people felt as if the king or lord himself was watching everything that happened in his land.

In times of war, the castle was a safe base for the lord's supporters as they fought their enemies.

The commander of Château-Gaillard was Baron Roger de Lacy. If he had kept a diary of the siege, this is what he might have written.

July 1203

The French are coming! My spies tell me King Philip's army will be here within the week. I have fewer than 200 fighting men; the French have many times that number. If we face them on the battlefield, we will be cut to pieces. Our only hope is to fight from inside the castle. My men are searching the countryside for the food and weapons we need. King John's orders are to defend the castle at all costs. I pray God will give us the strength to succeed.

Hoarding or hourde

Fortified bridge to main castle

Stable

Treadmill to operate crane

Bastion defending main approach to castle

The site

The best places to build a castle were on a hill, at the edge of a cliff, or overlooking the sea or a river. These natural defenses made direct attack almost impossible. Château-Gaillard was built on a bend of the River Seine. It was thought that it could withstand any attack.

River Seine

Village (Les Andelys)

Keep

Fortified bridges

Cliff

Inner bailey

Outer bailey

Outwork or bastion

Inner gateway with portcullis

Keep or donjon

Inner curtain wall

Outer curtain wall

Outer bailey or enceinte

Mill tower

Drawbridge

Building the castle

More than 6,000 workers helped to build Château-Gaillard. Amazingly, it took them not much more than a year (1197–1198).

Scaffolding made from wooden poles tied together

Walls of iron, walls of butter

According to legend, King Philip of France boasted that he could capture Château-Gaillard even if the walls were made of iron.

King Richard replied that he could defend it even if they were made of butter!

The Siege Begins

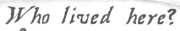

*A*ttacking a strongly built castle was not easy. The massive stone walls could stand up to most weapons, and the defenders had a commanding view of the countryside all around. Attackers might try to take the castle by surprise, or to bribe the defenders out by offering them money. Only once everything else had been tried did the attackers settle down to besiege the castle.

What is a siege?
The purpose of siege warfare was to cut off the castle from the outside world. The besieging army surrounded the castle so that no one could get in or out. They knew that if the defenders could not get food into the castle they would have to surrender or starve.

Stocking up
When a siege was expected, men were sent out from the castle to buy, borrow, or steal all the food they could find. Then they raised the drawbridges and barred the gates to keep the attackers out. If the defenders were well prepared, they might be able to last out until help came, or until the attackers gave up.

Who lived here?

The lord and his family

Officials: reeve, clerks, priest, marshal

Fighting men: knights, archers, crossbowmen

Entertainers: jugglers, jesters, musicians

August 1203

The French are here. The first of King Philip's soldiers arrived yesterday, and now they have us surrounded. They hoped to take us by surprise, but we were ready. All my men were safely inside the castle walls, and our gates were shut and barricaded. Many of the local villagers have taken shelter here as well. They know this is the strongest fortress ever built.

Today Philip's messenger called on us to surrender. If he'd been closer I would have laughed in his face. We will never surrender! It can only be a matter of weeks before King John arrives with an army that will send the French running for their lives.

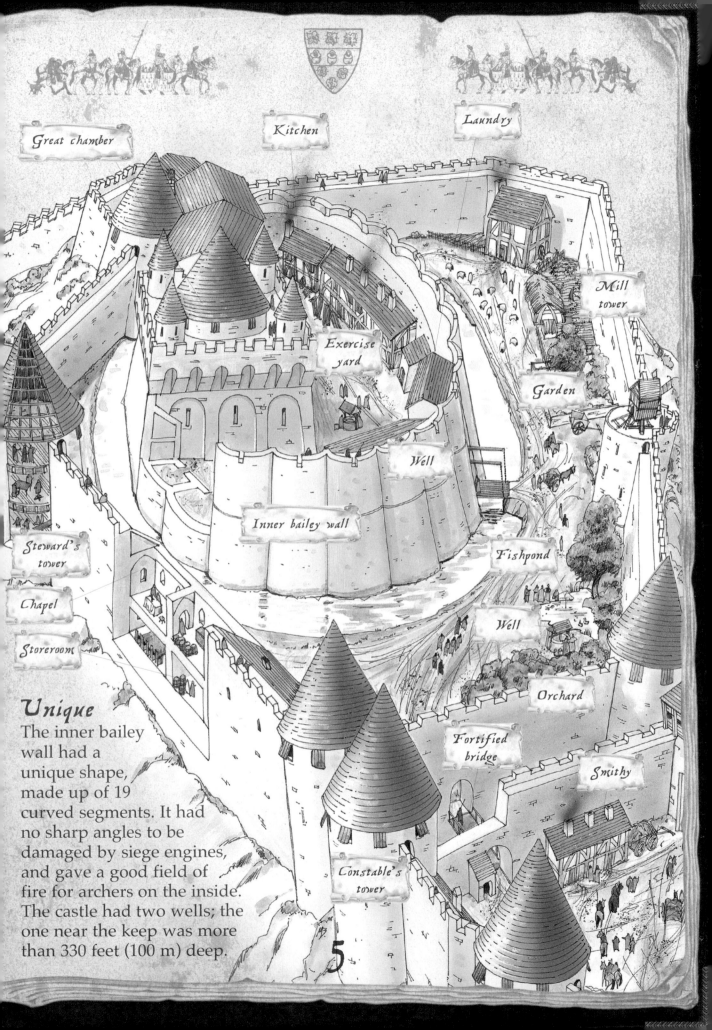

Great chamber

Kitchen

Laundry

Mill tower

Exercise yard

Garden

Well

Inner bailey wall

Fishpond

Steward's tower

Well

Chapel

Orchard

Storeroom

Fortified bridge

Smithy

Unique

The inner bailey wall had a unique shape, made up of 19 curved segments. It had no sharp angles to be damaged by siege engines, and gave a good field of fire for archers on the inside. The castle had two wells; the one near the keep was more than 330 feet (100 m) deep.

Constable's tower

5

Castle Life

Castles weren't just fortresses to be defended or attacked; they were also places where people lived and worked. They were the homes of powerful lords and ladies, sometimes even kings and queens. Inside their massive walls and towers were all the comforts that such important people expected.

Personal hygiene

Medieval people did their best to keep clean—we know that they washed their hands before meals, for example. But the effort of drawing water from the well and heating it meant that even important people bathed only occasionally.

September 1203

Curse the day that King John put the wretched Earl of Pembroke in charge of the army sent to relieve us!

The plan was to strike the French army from two sides at once. One force was to attack overland while the other sailed up the river and attacked from behind. But by the time the English ships arrived, the French had already defeated the land attack. Then their soldiers turned around and fought off the attack from the river.

Now we will have to wait weeks, or even months, for King John to come to our aid a second time.

Holding the fort

When Château-Gaillard was besieged, its owner King John was not there. He was in Rouen, the capital of Normandy, about 25 miles (40 km) away. It was usual for kings to move around, visiting different parts of their lands.

When the lord of a castle wasn't at home, a trusted lieutenant stayed behind with a garrison of soldiers. A castle could never be left undefended!

John sent the Earl of Pembroke with an army to try to relieve the castle, but did not go there himself.

Solar (private upstairs room)

Library

Storerooms

The lord's bed
After his horses and armor, a lord's bed was usually his most valuable possession. It was certainly the most expensive piece of furniture in the castle.

Master bedroom

Wardrobe

Bedroom

Spinning and weaving rooms

Home comforts
The living quarters in a castle were not the empty rooms with bare stone walls that we see today. Walls were neatly plastered and either painted or hung with expensive tapestries.

Meat is hung in the roof space, where it will be cured (dried and preserved) by smoke from the fire.

The rich have feather beds; ordinary beds are filled with straw. Curtains keep out the draft.

Brewing

Poultry

Hens and geese were kept for the eggs they laid. But if they stopped laying they were soon cooked and eaten.

Wattle and daub

Ordinary buildings were made of oak frames, filled in with panels of "wattle and daub." Wattles are made by weaving together rods and strips of oak. Daub is a kind of plaster made from clay and straw, sometimes with lime or cow dung. The daub makes the walls reasonably waterproof.

Thatch

Wattle

Oak frame

Daub

Hunting and hawking

Nobles enjoyed hunting both for food and for sport. Deer and wild boar were hunted with dogs. Small game was hunted with specially trained hawks or falcons, and this sport was considered suitable for ladies as well as gentlemen. When they were not hunting, the hawks' or falcons' heads were covered with hoods to keep them calm.

Hood

Perch

Jesses (leather straps to attach a leash)

Gauntlet

Thatched roofs give excellent insulation, provided they are kept in good repair.

The smith's assistant pumps the bellows to keep the fire burning brightly.

The blacksmith
A prosperous farm might have its own blacksmith. His duties included shoeing horses, making strakes (tires) for wheels, and making or repairing tools.

A few weeks later

Another day of disappointment! News has reached us that King John cannot send any more troops to fight off the French. It seems he has more important battles to fight elsewhere. Now all we can do is sit and wait. King Philip must realize that Château-Gaillard is too strong to be captured by force. His only chance is to starve us into surrender. But we have gardens and livestock inside the castle walls, and stores of food to last us many months. My only worry is the villagers who are sheltering here. We cannot feed them as well. That is a problem I must do something about before it is too late.

Scythe for mowing

Well

Plow

Churn

Farm animals
Pig meat was either eaten fresh as pork, or turned into ham and bacon, which last much longer. Cows, goats, and sheep were kept mostly for the milk they gave. It was only when the winter came, and there was not enough food to feed the animals, that they were killed and eaten as meat.

9

Making Do

Pot-hooks

Cooking pot

Piglet roasting on spit

At the start of a siege, people living in the castle probably ate quite well. The storerooms and cellars were still full of grain and flour to make fresh bread. The castle grounds were teeming with livestock which gave them milk, meat, and eggs. And, if it was summer, there were fresh vegetables and fruit growing in the gardens and orchards.

Salting meat

The usual way of preserving meat through the winter was to salt it. The salt dried the meat by sucking all the moisture out of it.

October 1203

We are now two months into the siege. We have beaten off all the French attacks so far, but they have cut off our supplies of food. From now on we must save as much food as we can. That is why today I gave orders that most of the villagers who were sheltering here be turned out of the castle. They were fearful that the French would kill them — but to my surprise their soldiers let them pass. It will be a long, hard winter for them, but what else can we do?

The French have dug a line of trenches around the castle. Now it seems they are building siege towers to attack our walls. But the castle is strong and we can hold them off.

Pottery jar for
wine, oil, etc.

Brushwood
for fire

Pastrycook

Geese from the
castle yard

Water from
the well

Making it last

As the siege went on, the castle cooks' job became more difficult, because there was no way of keeping food fresh. Butter and cheese made from milk kept quite well, although sometimes the cheese grew too hard to cut. Fruit and vegetables had to be pickled or dried if they were to last more than a couple of weeks. Meat was smoked or salted, but this did not stop it going rotten, so the cooks might need to use strong spices and herbs to hide any nasty taste. Sometimes, by the end of a long siege, the defenders had nothing left to eat but moldy bread and rats.

The medieval menu

In peacetime, wealthy people ate mostly meat, including game which they had hunted themselves. The poor lived mostly on things made from grain: bread, porridge, and weak beer.

11

The Poor in War

Most castles had a village nearby. The people who lived there grew the crops which fed the people at the castle. They were serfs, which meant that they had very few rights and were almost owned by the local lord. In return, it was, in theory, his duty to protect them when they were in danger.

The peasants' lot

It's always the poor that suffer! In wartime, soldiers often attacked villages and towns, and took food and anything else of value that they found. Sometimes they even burned down the houses. The villagers could not fight back, so they sheltered in the castle grounds. But feeding hundreds of villagers meant that the castle's food ran out more quickly. Because of this, villagers were often driven out of the castle—and that is what Roger de Lacy did. He called them "useless mouths."

> *December 1203*
>
> *The siege has lasted four months now, and as we get deeper into winter our supplies of food grow low. Some weeks ago I had to turn the remaining villagers out of the castle. This time the French did not let them pass. They drove them back to the castle gates, but I dared not let them in again. We cannot afford to feed useless mouths! The poor wretches were stuck between us and the French. They had no food, no water, and no shelter from the freezing winter weather. It was only after many had died from starvation and cold that Philip let them pass. Not that they had anywhere to go—their homes have probably been burned down.*

Soldiers loot the village below the castle

Those who resist are likely to be killed

12

Peasant life

The life of a medieval peasant was tough. They worked long hours in the fields just to keep themselves from going hungry, and a portion of what they grew was taken by the lord of the manor as rent.

Lost in no-man's-land

If the besiegers wouldn't let them pass, then the wretched men, women, and children turned out of the castle were trapped in the open without food or shelter. Their only hope was to stay alive until one side or the other finally took pity on them.

Fighting Men

There were very few full-time soldiers in the Middle Ages. Kings and other lords had a small band of troops to protect them, and every castle had a garrison of trained fighting men who kept it safe from surprise attack. It was only in times of war that large armies were raised.

Leaving home to train as a knight

Knights and foot soldiers

Knights were the elite fighters in a medieval army. They rode horses, wore armor, and could fight either on horseback or on foot. They were highly trained and spent a lot of time practicing their fighting skills.

Archers were also highly skilled, but, like ordinary foot soldiers, most of them were only called up into the army when they were needed. In peacetime they were farmers who worked on the land. Their fields had to be plowed, seeds sown, and crops harvested. If any of those things weren't done, people would starve. Sometimes a siege had to be called off simply because it was time for the attacking army to return to their fields to work.

Haqueton (padded jacket)

Longbow made of yew wood

Quiver of arrows

Archer

14

Practice sword

Practice shield

Knights were men from well-off families who had been trained to fight from an early age. They began learning with wooden swords and shields.

Late January 1204

We are now starting our sixth month trapped inside the castle. The lack of food makes everyone weak and bad-tempered. At least we have water—the late King Richard had the wisdom to build two wells inside the castle. But many of us are falling ill and do not have the strength to recover.

We must try to hold out until the spring. Then Philip will have to let most of his men return to their farms to plant their crops. But now we hear that his troops are flattening the rocky ground between their trenches and the castle walls. That can only mean one thing: They are preparing to strike.

Steel helmet

Chain mail

Pike

A knight's armor was made to measure by a highly skilled armorer. It was very expensive.

Attack and Defense

The attackers could not afford to keep up the siege forever. Once the defenders had been weakened by hunger and disease, the attacking forces might finally try to take the castle by storm. This is what Philip did at Château-Gaillard, after the siege had dragged on all winter. It was very unusual for medieval armies to fight through the winter—Philip must have been determined to get his way.

Drawbridge

Siege tower covered with wet animal hides to protect against fire and arrows

Pavises (archery shields)

Moat

February 1204

The final battle for Château-Gaillard has begun. Early this morning the French mounted an attack on our outer walls. Their archers fired off hundreds of arrows to drive us from the battlements. Under cover of these arrows, their soldiers began moving siege towers and other machines over the ground that they have flattened in the past weeks. With no thought for their own lives, my archers fired back and many Frenchmen were killed. But by the end of the day their towers were in place and their machines were ready to fire. We can only hope that the strength of these mighty walls will be too much for them.

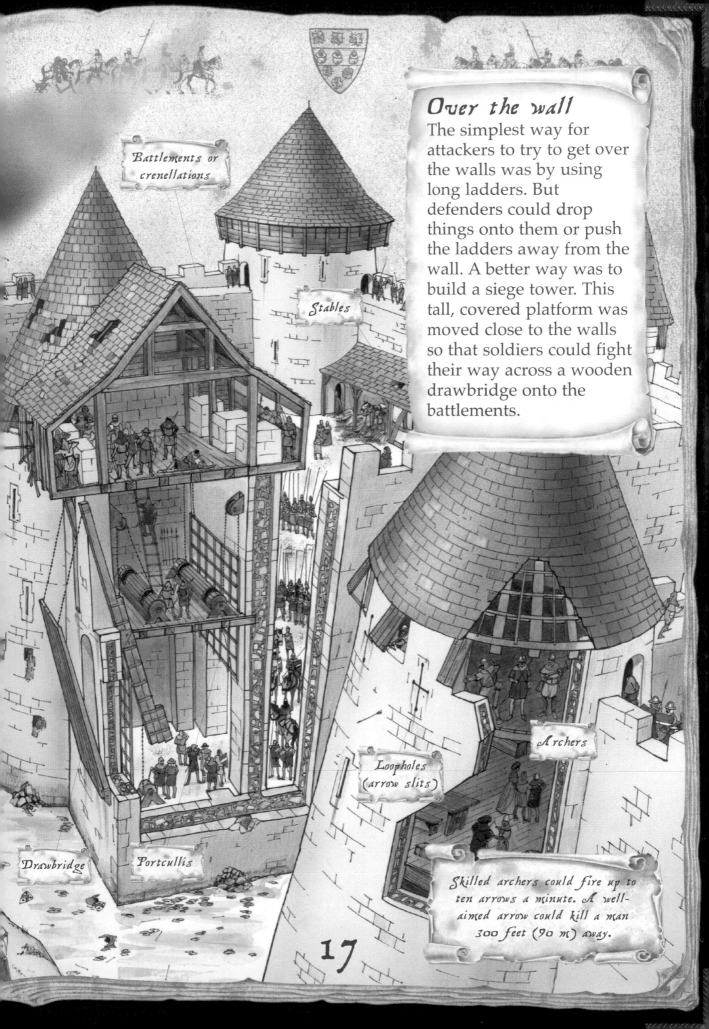

Battlements or
crenellations

Stables

Over the wall

The simplest way for
attackers to try to get over
the walls was by using
long ladders. But
defenders could drop
things onto them or push
the ladders away from the
wall. A better way was to
build a siege tower. This
tall, covered platform was
moved close to the walls
so that soldiers could fight
their way across a wooden
drawbridge onto the
battlements.

Archers

Loopholes
(arrow slits)

Drawbridge

Portcullis

Skilled archers could fire up to
ten arrows a minute. A well-
aimed arrow could kill a man
300 feet (90 m) away.

17

Bombardment

Castle walls were immensely strong, up to 10 feet (3 m) thick. It was not easy to break them down, but it could be done. Before cannons were invented, army engineers built huge siege engines—machines made from wood and ropes, which could fling heavy missiles a surprisingly long way. Mangonels and trebuchets throwing heavy stones were the most common siege engines. The attackers used them to batter the castle wall, hoping to weaken it until eventually part of it fell down.

One week later

Today is the sixth day that the French have battered our outer walls with rocks from their siege engines. But in spite of all their efforts, not the slightest crack has appeared. No wonder that this afternoon they loaded one of their engines with the rotting bodies of two dead horses. Then they hurled them over the wall into the outer bailey. Perhaps they have finally realized that they are wasting their time trying to smash through our wall. Instead they hope to infect us with some monstrous disease from the rotting horses. That will fail as well, I trust. A few more weeks and they will give up and go away—if we can only last out that long.

The ballista

The ballista, first invented by the ancient Greeks, was like a huge crossbow, firing giant arrows or "bolts."

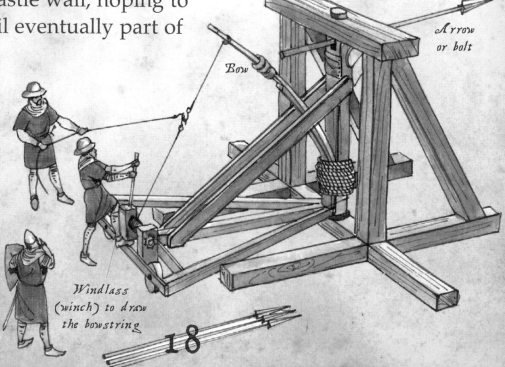

Bow

Arrow or bolt

Windlass (winch) to draw the bowstring

18

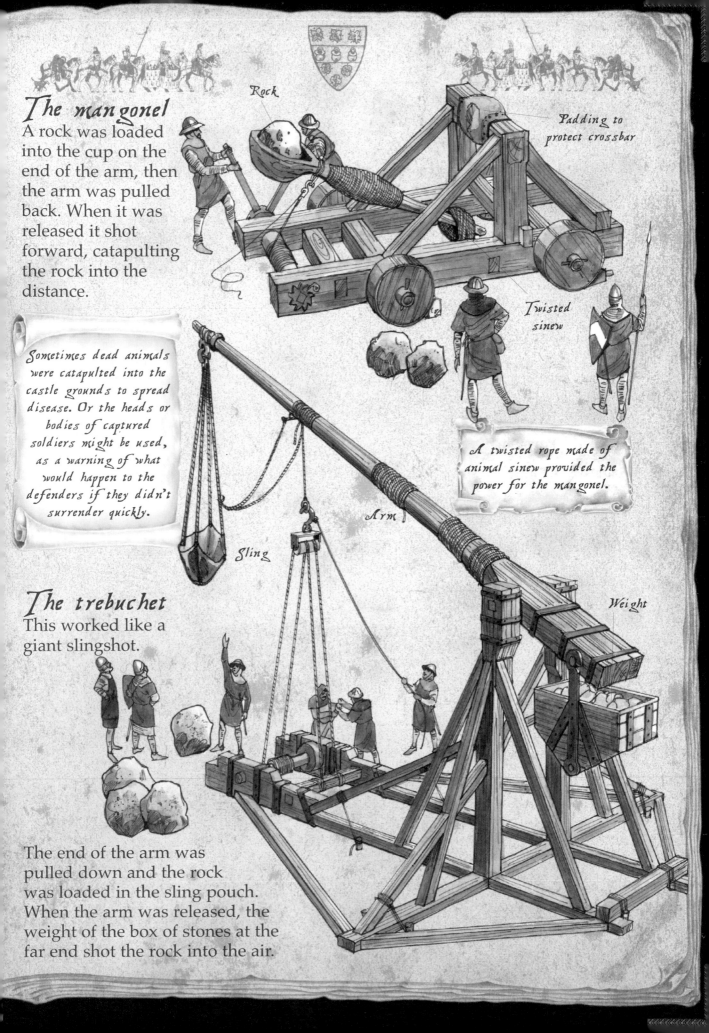

The mangonel

A rock was loaded into the cup on the end of the arm, then the arm was pulled back. When it was released it shot forward, catapulting the rock into the distance.

Rock

Padding to protect crossbar

Twisted sinew

Sometimes dead animals were catapulted into the castle grounds to spread disease. Or the heads or bodies of captured soldiers might be used, as a warning of what would happen to the defenders if they didn't surrender quickly.

A twisted rope made of animal sinew provided the power for the mangonel.

Sling

Arm

Weight

The trebuchet

This worked like a giant slingshot.

The end of the arm was pulled down and the rock was loaded in the sling pouch. When the arm was released, the weight of the box of stones at the far end shot the rock into the air.

Mining the Walls

*E*ven after weeks of bombardment by mangonels and trebuchets, a castle wall might still not fall. That's why attackers often mined underneath it as well. The idea was to weaken the wall's foundations until part of it fell down. Philip decided to use this method to get into the advance bastion—the separate, small castle that guarded the entrance to Château-Gaillard.

Sappers

The soldiers who dug mines were called sappers. They were usually men who had worked in lead or gold mines. Any kind of mining was dangerous, because the roof could easily fall in and kill everyone inside. But undermining a castle wall was even worse, because the defenders were trying to kill you while you did it. They might flood the mine with water and drown the miners. Or they might dig a tunnel of their own (a countermine) so they could go down and drive the miners out.

Two days later

I never thought it possible! Today part of the wall of the outer bastion collapsed. The French sappers had tunneled underneath it without our knowing. Yesterday they set fire to the wooden props supporting it. Even then the wall stood firm. But this morning their siege machines struck the undermined wall with one boulder after another, and finally it fell. Before the French could scramble in over the rubble, I gave orders to set fire to everything in the outer bastion. In the smoke and confusion we retreated to the outer bailey of the main castle. Its walls are higher and stronger, and we should be safe here. We have lost a battle, but I know we can still win the war.

Munitions

Arrowheads were made in many different styles, from narrow "bodkins" to wide heads with barbs. Some were specially hardened and may have been able to pierce chain mail.

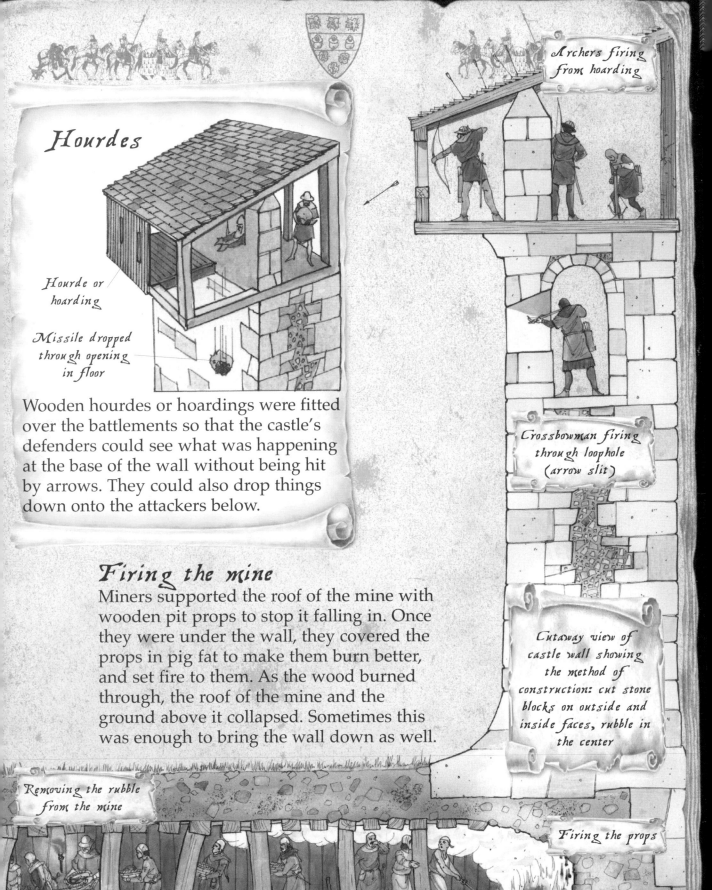

Hourdes

Hourde or hoarding

Missile dropped through opening in floor

Wooden hourdes or hoardings were fitted over the battlements so that the castle's defenders could see what was happening at the base of the wall without being hit by arrows. They could also drop things down onto the attackers below.

Firing the mine

Miners supported the roof of the mine with wooden pit props to stop it falling in. Once they were under the wall, they covered the props in pig fat to make them burn better, and set fire to them. As the wood burned through, the roof of the mine and the ground above it collapsed. Sometimes this was enough to bring the wall down as well.

Archers firing from hoarding

Crossbowman firing through loophole (arrow slit)

Cutaway view of castle wall showing the method of construction: cut stone blocks on outside and inside faces, rubble in the center

Removing the rubble from the mine

Firing the props

21

Praying for Help

Castles in Christian countries had at least one chapel. In larger castles there were often two. The lord and his family worshipped in a small private chapel close to their rooms. This could be highly decorated, with painted walls, gold crosses, and candlesticks, and sometimes even stained-glass windows. Everyone else went to services in a bigger chapel, which might be somewhere in the castle grounds. This would be more plainly decorated than the private chapel.

The castle priest

Castles had their own priests who said Mass every day of the week. Priests were important also because they could read and write; many people at this time couldn't even write their own names. Part of the priest's job was reading and explaining the Bible to those who couldn't read it for themselves. He might also help the lord with the many letters and documents he had to deal with.

Religion

Christianity was the main religion in Europe, but Islam was the chief religion in the Middle East. There was longstanding warfare at this time between the followers of these two religions—but there were also plenty of wars between people of the same religion.

The beginning of the end

At Château-Gaillard the main castle chapel was built against the wall of the outer bailey. Inside the chapel there was a "garderobe," or toilet. The waste from the garderobe dropped down through a space, or chute, in the wall and emptied to the outside. It is said that some French soldiers climbed up the garderobe chute into the chapel. Then they climbed out into the outer bailey through a chapel window and let down the drawbridge for the rest of the French troops.

22

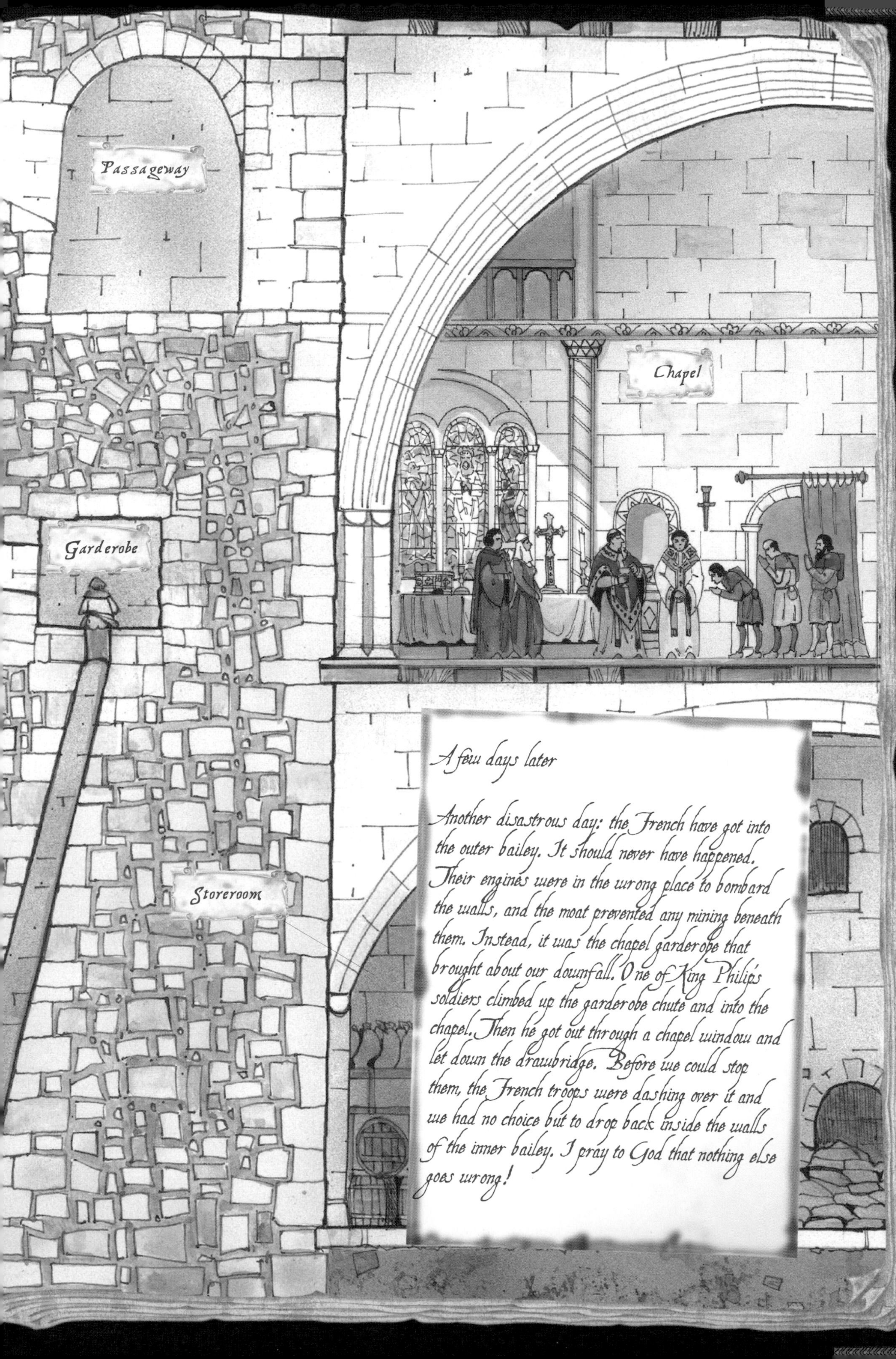

Passageway

Chapel

Garderobe

Storeroom

A few days later

Another disastrous day: the French have got into the outer bailey. It should never have happened. Their engines were in the wrong place to bombard the walls, and the moat prevented any mining beneath them. Instead, it was the chapel garderobe that brought about our downfall. One of King Philip's soldiers climbed up the garderobe chute and into the chapel. Then he got out through a chapel window and let down the drawbridge. Before we could stop them, the French troops were dashing over it and we had no choice but to drop back inside the walls of the inner bailey. I pray to God that nothing else goes wrong!

Hope Is Fading

Weakened by hunger and disease, seeing their walls battered and undermined, Roger's men must have known the end was near.

Mangonel

Siege tower

French sappers in mine

24

Trebuchet

Winching down the
arm of the trebuchet

Loading
the sling

Walls within walls

Château-Gaillard was what is called a "concentric
castle," with one set of walls inside another. First
the attacking troops had to fight their way into the
advanced bastion guarding the entrance. Then they
had to get across to the outer bailey of the main
castle, and from there to the inner bailey. Even then
the defenders could still retreat to the huge stone
tower called the keep. It was an immensely strong
fortress, but it was not unbreakable.

Siege engines

Extra-large siege towers and powerful trebuchets were sometimes given nicknames. A trebuchet used at the siege of Acre (1189–1191) was called *Malvoisin*, which means "Bad Neighbor," in medieval French.

Sappers digging a mine

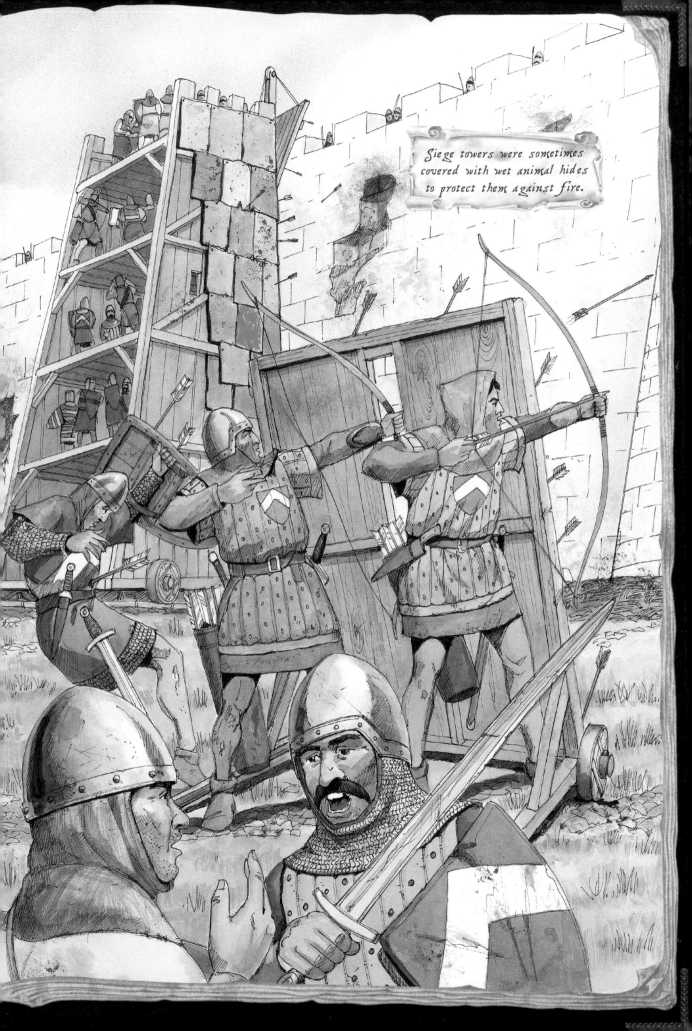

Siege towers were sometimes covered with wet animal hides to protect them against fire.

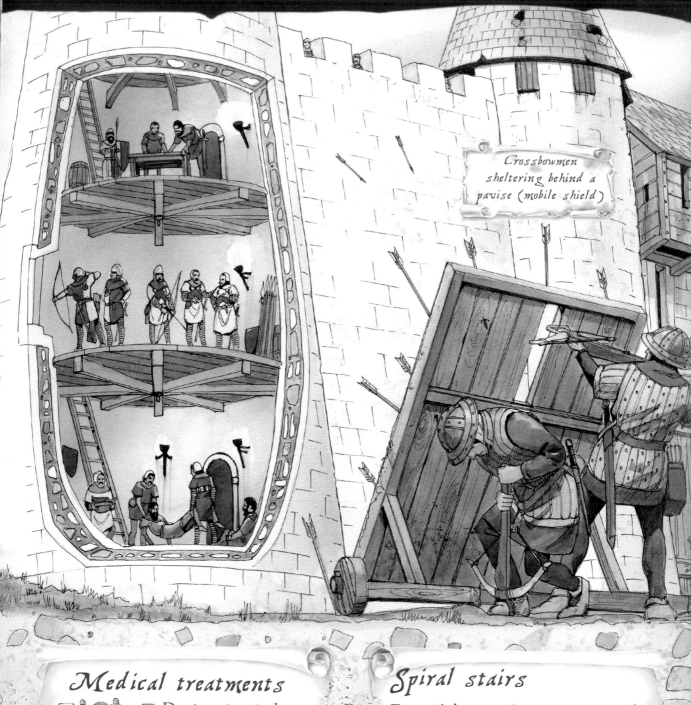

Crossbowmen sheltering behind a pavise (mobile shield)

Medical treatments

Doctors treated disease with herbal remedies and bloodletting, but the importance of good hygiene was not understood at this time. Often more people died from disease than from the fighting.

Spiral stairs

Even if the attackers got inside the castle keep, they had to fight their way up spiral staircases. This was hard because the defender was higher up and could bring his sword down on top of them.

Cutaway view

English soldiers
in countermine

25

1 March 1204

We have done our best, but we cannot hold out much longer. Our food has almost run out, and the men are weak and suffering from many illnesses.

Philip's sappers have dug another tunnel. This time we dug a countermine of our own and drove them out. But our walls are bound to have been weakened by the mining. King John must have heard of the great troubles we are facing, but it seems we are on our own.

Taken by Storm

Many sieges ended without any hand-to-hand fighting when one side or the other decided that they could no longer carry on. But sometimes the attackers did manage to break through all the defenses and finally come face to face with the castle defenders. Then the fighting could be fierce and bloody.

6 March 1207

It is all over. The mining had indeed weakened the inner bailey wall, and today the constant bombardment brought part of it down. Those of my men who were still fit and able rushed in to defend the gap. But in their panic they forgot the two tunnels under the wall. The cunning French sent soldiers down their tunnel and into our countermine that joined it. The next thing we knew, they were up in the inner bailey and attacking us from behind. We fought well but were outnumbered, and could not even manage to make our final escape to the castle keep. We are now prisoners of the French.

Moat

Armor

A knight's armor at this time was made of chain mail—plate armor came later, in the 14th century. The two common types of helmet were the conical helmet with nasal (nose piece), and the more modern great helm, which completely enclosed the head. Foot soldiers had much less protection.

Surrender

Both sides knew that if no army came to the rescue of those inside, then the attackers would win, if they waited long enough. It was the defenders' duty not to surrender for at least 40 days. After that they could surrender with honor. Château-Gaillard held out for about seven months, from August 1203 (we don't know the exact date) to March 6, 1204.

Surrender or die

Once it was clear that defeat was inevitable, the best thing the defenders could do was to surrender. Then there was a good chance that they would be allowed to live. If they fought to the bitter end, they might be shown no mercy at all.

7 March 1204

I have spent my first night as a prisoner agonizing over what has happened. Could I have done more? I think not. At the end I had only 140 men left, and many of those were injured or too ill to fight. Even the fit ones were close to starving and almost asleep on their feet. Few had any strength to continue the fight. They gave everything they could to keep Château-Gaillard in the hands of England and King John. But no one came to help us. Now I can only hope that King Philip will show mercy and allow my brave men to live.

What happened next?

The valiant defenders of Château-Gaillard were spared by the French king and ransomed. King John himself paid 1,000 marks of silver to ransom Roger de Lacy. King John lost Normandy and most of his lands in France. No wonder his nickname was John Lackland.

Roger de Lacy surrenders his sword

A herald announces that the garrison has surrendered

Useful Words

armorer a metalworker who made armor.

bailey the area of ground inside a castle's walls. Château-Gaillard had two sets of walls, forming an inner and an outer bailey.

ballista a siege engine resembling a giant crossbow.

bastion a small fortress attached to a larger one. Because Château-Gaillard could only be attacked from one direction, a bastion was built to protect that side.

battlements the top part of a castle's walls, usually with a walkway on the inside where defenders could stand.

curtain wall a strong outer wall surrounding a castle, with towers along it for defense.

drawbridge a bridge, usually over a moat or ditch, which can be raised and lowered.

garderobe a medieval toilet. The waste dropped through a chute in the castle wall.

garrison a troop of soldiers stationed in a castle to protect it from attack.

hoarding or **hourde** a wooden shelter for defenders, overhanging the battlements.

keep the main tower of a castle; the final place for the defenders to retreat to. The rest of the castle's walls were there to protect the keep.

knight a highly trained fighting man who rode a horse and wore armor. He could fight on horseback or on foot. He usually came from a wealthy family, and owned land.

mangonel a siege machine made from wood and twisted ropes; a kind of catapult.

Middle Ages a modern name for the period between about AD 1000 and 1500.

mining or **undermining** digging tunnels under the foundations of a wall to weaken it and help bring it down.

missile any kind of weapon that is thrown in some way.

moat a deep ditch, usually filled with water, surrounding all or part of a castle.

portcullis a heavy grille, sliding up and down in grooves, that can be used to close a gateway.

ransom to pay money for a prisoner to be released. This was a normal part of warfare in the Middle Ages.

serf a person who farmed land but did not own it. Serfs had few rights and were not much more than slaves to the lords who owned the land.

siege the process of trying to capture a castle or town by surrounding it with troops so that it was totally cut off from the outside world.

siege engine any kind of machine used to attack a castle during a siege.

siege tower a wooden tower that was moved up to a castle's walls so that attacking soldiers could climb across to the battlements.

trebuchet a siege engine that worked like a giant slingshot. It was bigger than a mangonel and was developed much later.

trench a narrow ditch, usually with a bank of earth in front of it, where soldiers can shelter from attackers.

Index